J. C. RYLE
SERMONS
TO
CHILDREN

Seven Biblical Lessons for Children

Register This New Book

Benefits of Registering*

- ✓ FREE **replacements** of lost or damaged books
- ✓ FREE **audiobook** – *Pilgrim's Progress,* audiobook edition
- ✓ FREE information about new titles and other **freebies**

www.anekopress.com/new-book-registration

*See our website for requirements and limitations.

J. C. RYLE
SERMONS
TO
CHILDREN

Seven Biblical Lessons for Children

J. C. RYLE

ANEKO
PRESS

We love hearing from our readers. Please contact us at www.anekopress.com/questions-comments with any questions, comments, or suggestions.

J. C. Ryle Sermons to Children
© 2021 by Aneko Press
All rights reserved. First edition 1880.
Updated edition copyright 2021.

Please do not reproduce, store in a retrieval system, or transmit in any form or by any means – electronic, mechanical, photocopying, recording, or otherwise, without written permission from the publisher. Please contact us via www.AnekoPress.com for reprint and translation permissions.

Scripture notated NKJV is taken from the New King James Version®. Copyright © 1982 by Thomas Nelson. Used by permission. All rights reserved.

Unless otherwise noted, scripture quotations from The Authorized (King James) Version. Rights in the Authorized Version in the United Kingdom are vested in the Crown. Reproduced by permission of the Crown's patentee, Cambridge University Press.

Cover Designer: Jonathan Lewis
Editor: Paul Miller

Aneko Press

www.anekopress.com

Aneko Press, Life Sentence Publishing, and our logos are trademarks of
Life Sentence Publishing, Inc.
203 E. Birch Street
P.O. Box 652
Abbotsford, WI 54405

JUVENILE NONFICTION / Religion / Christianity

Paperback ISBN: 978-1-62245-784-7
eBook ISBN: 978-1-62245-785-4

10 9 8 7 6 5 4 3 2 1

Available where books are sold

Contents

Ch. 1: The Two Bears 1

Ch. 2: Children Walking in Truth 15

Ch. 3: Little and Wise 33

Ch. 4: No More Crying! 47

Ch. 5: The Happy Little Girl 61

Ch. 6: Seeking the Lord Early 65

Ch. 7: Boys and Girls Playing 83

J. C. Ryle – A Brief Biography 89

Other Similar Titles 95

Chapter 1

The Two Bears

And he went up from thence unto Bethel: and as he was going up by the way, there came forth little children out of the city, and mocked him, and said unto him, Go up, thou bald head; go up, thou bald head. And he turned back, and looked on them, and cursed them in the name of the LORD. And there came forth two she bears out of the wood, and tare forty and two children of them.
– 2 Kings 2:23-24

Dear children, did you ever see a bear? Perhaps not. There are not as many wild bears in this country now as there used to be. You can see some bears in some wild animal shows or in cages in zoos, but you do not usually see them in the woods and fields. So perhaps you never saw a bear. A bear is a large, shaggy animal with large teeth and claws, and is very strong. It will kill sheep, lambs, calves, and goats – and eat them. When it is very hungry, it will even attack men, women, or children and tear them to pieces! Female bears that have little cubs are particularly fierce and cruel. How thankful we should be that we can walk around in most of our forests without fear of being caught by a bear!

Now I am going to tell you a story about a godly man, two bears, and some children. It is a story out of the Bible, so you can be sure that it is all true. Stories in other books are often only make-believe and tell us things that never really happened. Stories out of the Bible, though, are true in every word. Never forget that!

Many hundred years ago, there lived a godly man whose name was Elisha. First he was the servant to a famous prophet of God named Elijah. After Elijah was taken up to heaven in a chariot of fire, Elisha was appointed to be a prophet in his place.

From that time until his death, he was a very great and a very useful man. He did many miracles. He used to go up and down the land of Israel reproving sinners and teaching people how to serve God. In some places he had schools, called "schools of the prophets." In this way he became famous all over the country. All people knew Elisha, and all godly people loved him.

One day, not long after Elijah had been taken up to heaven, Elisha went to a place called Bethel, where there was a school. Perhaps he went to see how the school was doing and whether it was doing any good. All schools need to be looked after and examined, and it does them good to be examined. Only bad boys and girls dislike being asked what they have learned.

Now as this good old man, Elisha, got near Bethel, a very sad thing happened. A large number of little children came out of the town and behaved very badly. They began to mock Elisha and call him names. Instead of respecting him like good children should have done, they made fun of him and said bad things. "Go on up, you bald head!" they cried, "Go on up, you bald head!"

They called him "bald head," I have no doubt, because the good prophet was bald in his old age and had no hair on his head. They said, "Go on up," I suppose, because his master Elijah had previously gone up to heaven, as everybody knew. They meant that Elisha had better go away after his master and not trouble them any more with his teaching. It was as if they were saying, "Go away and be gone! It is time for you to go up like your master did."

Just think for a moment how wicked these

children were! They lived in a town where they could have learned better things. There was a school of prophets at Bethel, but I am afraid they had not used their opportunities. They had loved play better than lessons. They had no business to mock Elisha and treat him so badly. He had done them no harm. He had never been unkind to them. He was a godly man, and one who was their best friend. Above all, they should not have said, "Go on up, and get away." Instead, they should have said, "Stay with us and teach us the way to heaven."

It is truly sad to see how wicked even little children can be. It is sad to see how sinful boys and girls may become, and what disrespectful and unkind things they will say, even when they live close to a school!

But what did Elisha do when these children behaved so badly? We are told that he turned around and looked at them with displeasure. They had probably often done the same thing before. It had become a habit with them that they would not stop. The time had come for them to be punished. We are told that Elisha then called down a curse on them in the name of the Lord.

You can be sure that Elisha did not fly into an angry passion and swear at the children as some bad men might have done. He was not a man to say that kind of thing. It only means that he solemnly pronounced God's anger and displeasure against them. He solemnly told them *in the name of the LORD* that God would certainly punish them, and that it was his duty as God's servant to say so. Elisha did not speak in anger. The judge at the court is not angry with the prisoner when he sentences him to be put in prison. When Elisha pronounced God's curse on these wicked children, he did it as God's appointed servant – firmly and faithfully. Undoubtedly, God told him what to do, and like an obedient servant, he did it.

What happened as soon as Elisha had spoken? At once two female bears came rushing out of the woods and attacked these wicked children, tearing and killing all they caught! Think what an awful surprise that must have been! How dreadfully frightened these children must have felt! What running, screaming, tumbling over one another, and crying for help there must have been! How sorry and ashamed of themselves they must have felt! But with many, it was too late. Before they could get within the walls of Bethel, the two bears had caught and killed forty-two little children! Forty-two little boys and girls that night never came home to Bethel alive! Forty-two little suppers were not eaten! Forty-two little beds were not slept in! Forty-two little funerals took place the next day! Some of the other children, I hope, got home safely and were not hurt, but I am sure they would never forget what they had seen. They would remember the two bears as long as they lived!

Now, dear children, this is a sad story, but it is a very useful and instructive one. Like everything else in the Bible, it was written for your good. It teaches lessons that boys and girls should never forget. Let me tell you what those lessons are.

1. God takes notice of what children do.
God took notice of the little children at Bethel and punished them for their wickedness. Remember, I beg of you, that God has not changed. He is still the same. He is taking notice of you every day.

I believe some people think that it does not matter how children behave, and that God only notices grown-up men and women. This is a very big mistake. The eyes of God are upon boys and girls, and He notices all they do! When they do right, He is pleased; and when they do wrong, He is displeased. Dear children, never forget this!

Let no one make you think that you are too young to serve God and that you can safely wait until you are grown-up men and women. This is not true. It is never too soon to become a Christian. As soon as you know right from wrong, you are old enough to begin taking the right way. As soon as you are old enough to be punished for doing wrong, you are old enough to give your heart to God and to follow Christ. The child who is old enough to be punished for swearing and telling lies is old enough to be taught to pray and read the Bible. The child who is big enough to displease God is also big enough to please Him. The child who is old enough to be tempted by the devil is old enough to have the grace of the Holy Spirit in his heart.

Children, no matter how little and young you are, God is always noticing you! He notices how you behave at home, how you behave at school, and how you behave at play. He notices whether you say your prayers or not, and how you say them. He notices whether you obey what your mother tells you, and how you behave when you are out of your mother's sight. He notices whether you are selfish or angry or tell lies or take what is not your own. In short, there is nothing about children that God does not notice.

I read in the Bible that when little Ishmael was almost dead with thirst in the wilderness, God heard the voice of the boy (Genesis 21:17). Notice that God listened to the child's prayer. I read that when Samuel was only a little boy, God spoke to him (1 Samuel 3). I read that when Abijah, the child of Jeroboam, was sick and dying, God said by the mouth of His prophet that *there is some good thing found in him toward the* Lord *God*

(1 Kings 14:13). Children, these things were written for your learning.

Now I will give you a piece of advice. Say to yourselves every morning when you get up, "God sees me! Let me live as in God's sight." God is always watching what you do and hearing what you say. It is all written down in His great books, and everything must be accounted for at the last day. It is written in the Bible, *Even a child is known by his doings* (Proverbs 20:11).

2. It is very wrong to mock godly people and despise God's Word.

The little children of Bethel mocked Elisha and called him "bald head." For doing so, they were terribly punished.

Dear children, as long as you live, make it a rule never to laugh at the Bible or to mock Christian people. This is one of the wickedest things you can do. It is pleasant to see boys and girls merry and happy. Youth is the time for laughter and merriment, but take care never to laugh at anything belonging to God. Whatever you laugh at, do not laugh at God's Word.

Some boys and girls, I am sorry to say, are very thoughtless about this. They think it is clever to make fun of those who read their Bibles, say their prayers, and listen to what is said at church. They laugh at other boys and girls who obey what their fathers and mothers say, and they try to corrupt them. Some, indeed, are so wicked that when they see other children trying to do what pleases God, they will point their fingers at them and taunt, "There goes a little saint!"

All this is very wrong and offends God exceedingly. There is One in heaven who sees these wicked children, and when He sees them, He is greatly displeased. We cannot wonder if such children become troublemakers and turn out badly. All who despise God's people despise God Himself. It is written, *Those who honor Me I will honor, and those who despise Me shall be lightly esteemed* (1 Samuel 2:30).

I read in the Bible that Ishmael was turned out of Abraham's house because he mocked Isaac, his little brother (Genesis 21:9-10). At the time when Ishmael did this, he was only a boy. But even though he was a boy, he was old enough to offend God by mocking and to cause himself and his mother much trouble.

Dear children, some of you might have godly fathers and mothers who tell you to read your Bibles and say your prayers. I hope that you never laugh at them behind their backs and mock what they tell you about God's Word. If you do this, you can be certain that you commit a great sin! It is written, *The eye that mocketh at his father, and despiseth to obey his mother, the ravens of the valley shall pick it out, and the young eagles shall eat it* (Proverbs 30:17).

3. Sin is certain to bring sorrow in the end.
Sin brought wounds and death to the little children of Bethel. It brought weeping and crying to the homes of their parents. If these wicked boys and girls had not displeased God, they would not have been torn apart by the bears.

Dear children, as long as you live, you will always see the same thing. Those who want to have their own way and run into sin are sooner or later certain to find themselves in trouble. This trouble might not come at once. It might not even come for many long years. But sooner or later, it is sure to come. There is a dreadful hell at last, and those who will continue sowing sin are certain in time to reap sorrow.

Adam and Eve ate the forbidden fruit in Eden, and what was the consequence? Sorrow! They were cast out of the garden with shame (Genesis 3).

The people before the flood continued eating and drinking and despising Noah's advice about the flood. And what was the consequence? Sorrow! The flood came, and they were all drowned (Genesis 7:20-23).

The people of Sodom and Gomorrah continued sinning in spite of Lot's warnings. And what was the consequence? Sorrow! The fire fell from heaven, and they were all burned up (Genesis 19: 24-25)!

Esau despised his birthright. And what was the consequence? Sorrow! He sought it afterward too late, with many tears (Hebrews 12:17).

The people of Israel would not obey God's command and go up into the land of Canaan when He commanded them. And what was the consequence? Sorrow! They wandered forty years in the wilderness (Joshua 5:6).

Achan would not obey the command of Joshua, but took money and hid it under his tent. And what was the consequence? Sorrow! He was found out and was publicly stoned to death (Joshua 7).

Judas, one of the twelve apostles, would not give his whole heart to Christ, but coveted money and betrayed his Master. And what was the consequence? Sorrow! The money did him no good and did not make him happy, and he hanged himself (Matthew 27:5)!

Ananias and Sapphira told a big lie to Peter and the apostles in order to be thought well of. And what was the consequence? Sorrow! They were both struck dead in one day (Acts 5:1-10)!

Dear children, remember these things to the end of your lives. *The wages of sin is death* (Romans 6:23).

Sin is certain to bring sorrow at last! Those who tell lies or steal or hurt others may not suffer for it at first, but their sin will surely find them out! Sooner or later, in this world or the next, those who sow sin, like these wicked children of Bethel, are sure to reap sorrow. *The way of transgressors is hard* (Proverbs 13:15).

Now I will conclude what I have been saying with three closing instructions. Consider them well, and take them to heart.

1. **In the first place, settle it in your minds that the way to be happy is to be holy in the sight of God.** If you will have your own way and follow sin, you are certain to have trouble and sorrow.

2. **If you want to be holy, ask the Lord Jesus Christ to make you holy and to put His Spirit into your hearts.** I know that you cannot make yourselves good. Your hearts are too weak and the world and the devil are too strong. But Jesus Christ can make you holy, and He is ready and willing to do so. He can give you new hearts and power to overcome sin.

Take Jesus Christ for your Shepherd and Friend. Cast your souls upon Him. Jesus, who died on the cross to save us, has a special care for little children. He says that He loves those who love Him, and those who seek Him early will find Him (Proverbs 8:17). Jesus said to let the little children come unto Him and not to keep them away (Matthew 19:14).

3. **If you want to be kept from the evil that is in the world, remember daily that God sees you – and live as in God's sight.** Never mock godly people or make fun of the Bible. Love those most who love God most, and choose for friends those who are God's friends. Hate sin of all kind. When sinners entice you, do not go along with them (Proverbs 1:10). Hate that which is evil. Cling to that which is good (Romans 12:9).

Dear children, if you live in this way, God will bless you, and you will find in the end that, like Mary, you have chosen the good part that cannot be taken from you (Luke 10:42).

Remember these things, and you will have learned something from "The Two Bears."

Chapter 2

Children Walking in Truth

I rejoiced greatly that I found of your children walking in truth. – 2 John 4

Beloved children, the book of the Bible from which my verse is taken is the shortest book in the Bible. It only has thirteen verses. As short as it is, though, it is full of important things, and I think the verse above is one of them.

This book is an epistle, or letter, written by the apostle John. He wrote it to a good Christian lady whom he knew. This lady had children, and some of them were the children spoken of in the verse.

It seems that John found some of this good lady's children at a place where he happened to go, and you see how well he found them behaving. He was able to write a good report of them to their mother, and that is the report of our verse: *I rejoiced greatly that I found of your children walking in truth.*

Now, dear children, there are only two things I want to tell you about from this verse. Some of you might be wondering, "What does *walking in truth* mean?" Others might be thinking, "Why did John rejoice so greatly?" I will try to answer these two questions. First, I will try to show you when it can be said that children walk in truth. Second, I will try to show you what the reasons were that made the apostle John rejoice so greatly.

Dear children, let me ask you one favor. Let me ask you to try to pay close attention. I will not make this long. Come then, and listen to what I have to tell you. May the Holy Spirit open your heart and bless what I say.

I. When can it be said that children walk in truth?

What does "walking" mean here? You must not think that it means to walk on our feet as you walk around outside. Rather, it means our way of behaving ourselves – our way of living. The Bible calls this "walking" because a person's life is just like a journey. From the time of our birth to the time of our death, we are always traveling and moving on. Life is a journey from the cradle to the grave, and because of that, a person's manner of living is often called his "walk."

But what does "walking in truth" mean? It means walking in the ways of true Bible religion, and not in the bad ways of this evil world. The world, I am sorry to tell you, is full of false ideas and untruths, and it is especially full of untruths about religion. They all come from our great enemy, the devil. The devil deceived Adam and Eve in Eden and made them sin by telling them an untruth. He told them they would not die if they ate the forbidden fruit – and that was untrue.

The devil is always at the same work now. He is always trying to make men, women, and children have false ideas about God and religion. He persuades them to believe that what is really evil is good, and what is really good is evil. He tries to convince them that serving God is not pleasant and that sin will do them no great harm. I am sad to say that vast numbers of people are deceived by him and believe these untruths.

However, those people who walk in truth are very different. They do not pay any attention to the false ideas that are in the world about religion. They follow the true way that God shows us in the Bible. No matter what others may do, their main desire is to please God and to be His true servants. This was the character of the children spoken of in the verse. John wrote home to their mother and said, "I found your children walking in truth."

Dear children, wouldn't you like to know whether you are walking in truth yourselves? Wouldn't you like to know the signs by which you can find it out? Listen while I try to set these characteristics before you in order. Listen and hear what I am going to say.

*1. Children who walk in truth
know the truth about sin.*

What is sin? Sin is breaking any command of God. To do anything that God says should not be done is sin. God is very holy and very pure, and every sin that is sinned greatly displeases Him. In spite of all this, though, most people in the world, both old and young, think very little about sin. Some try to say that they are not big sinners and do not often break God's commandments. Others say that sin is not such a terrible thing after all, and that God is not as particular and strict as some say He is. These are two great and dangerous mistakes.

Children who walk in truth think very differently. They have no such proud and strong feelings. They feel that they are full of sin, and this grieves and humbles them. They believe that sin is the abhorrent thing that God hates. They look upon sin as their greatest enemy and plague. They hate it more than anything on earth. There is nothing they so fully desire to be free from as sin.

Dear children, that is the first characteristic of walking in truth. Look at it. Think about it. Do you hate sin?

2. Children who walk in truth love the true Savior of sinners and follow Him.

There are few men and women who do not feel that they need to be saved in some way. They believe that after death comes the judgment, and they would like to be saved from that dreadful judgment.

But sadly, few of them will see that the Bible says there is only one Savior – Jesus Christ – and few go to Jesus Christ and ask Him to save them. Instead, they trust their own prayers, their own repentance, their own church attendance, the sacraments, their own goodness, or something of the kind. But these things, although useful in their place, cannot save anyone from hell. These are false ways of salvation. They cannot take away sin. They are not Christ.

Nothing can save you or me but Jesus Christ, who died for sinners on the cross. Only those who trust themselves entirely to Him have their sins forgiven and will go to heaven. Only these people will find that they have an Almighty Friend on the day of judgment. This is the true way to be saved.

Children who walk in truth have learned all this, and if you ask them what they put their trust in, they will answer, "Nothing but Christ!" They try to follow Jesus in the same way as lambs follow a good shepherd. Children who walk in truth love Jesus because they read in the Bible that He loved them and gave Himself for them.

Little children, that is the second characteristic of walking in truth. Look at it. Think about it. Do you love Christ?

3. Children who walk in truth serve God with a true heart.

I dare say that you know it is very possible to serve God with outward service only. Many do so. They will put on a serious face and pretend to be serious while they do not feel it. They will say beautiful prayers with their lips, yet do not mean what they say. They will sit in their places at church every Sunday, yet be thinking of other things all the time. Such service is outward service, and it is very wrong.

Bad children, I am sorry to say, are often guilty of this sin. They will say their prayers regularly when their parents make them – but not otherwise. They will seem to pay attention in church when their parents are watching them, but not at other times. Their hearts are far away.

Children who walk in truth are not like this. They have another spirit in them. Their desire is to be honest in all they do with God and to worship Him in spirit and in truth. When they pray, they try to be very sincere and to mean all the words they say. When they go to church, they try to be really serious and give their minds to what they hear. One of their main difficulties is that they cannot serve God more fully than they do.

Little children, that is the third characteristic of walking in truth. Look at it. Think about it. Is your heart false or true?

4. Children who walk in truth really try to do things right and true in the sight of God.
God has told us very plainly what He thinks is right. Nobody who reads the Bible with an honest heart can mistake this, but it is sad to see how few men and women care about pleasing God. Many people break His commandments continually and seem to think nothing of it. Some people will tell lies, swear, fight, cheat, and steal. Others use bad words, never pray to God at all, and never read their Bibles. Others are unkind to their family members or are lazy, gluttonous, angry, or selfish. No matter what people may choose to think, all of these things are very wicked and displeasing to the holy God.

Children who walk in truth are always trying to keep clear of bad ways. They take no pleasure in sinful things of any kind, and they dislike the company of those who do. Their great desire is to be like Jesus – holy, harmless, and separate from sinners (Hebrews 7:26). They try to be kind, gentle, sincere, obedient, honest, truthful, and good in all their ways. It saddens them that they are not more holy than they are.

Little children, that is the last characteristic I will give you of walking in truth. Look at it. Think about it. Are your actions right or wrong?

* * * *

Children, you have now heard some characteristics of walking in truth. I have tried to set them plainly before you. I hope you have understood them: knowing the truth about sin; loving the true Savior, Jesus Christ; serving God with a true heart; and doing things true and right in the sight of God. There they are – all four together. Think about them, I ask you. Ask yourself this: "What am I doing at this very time? Am I walking in truth?"

I am sure that many boys and girls know well what answer they should give. God knows, too, for He sees your hearts clearly! Children, the all-seeing

God sends you a question now: "Are you walking in truth?"

Why should you not walk in the truth? Thousands of dear children have walked in truth already, and have found it pleasant. The way has been traveled by many little feet before your own. Thousands of boys and girls are walking in truth at this moment, and there is still room for more. Dear children, ask yourself now, "Why should I not walk in the truth?"

II. What are some of the reasons why John rejoiced to find this lady's children walking in truth?

The verse says, *I rejoiced greatly*. Why did he rejoice? There must have been some good reasons. John was not a man to rejoice without cause. Listen, dear children, and you will hear what those reasons were.

1. John rejoiced because he was a good man himself.

All good people like to see others, as well as themselves, walking in truth. I dare say you have heard how the angels in heaven rejoice when they see one sinner repenting. Some of you, no doubt, have read it in the fifteenth chapter of Luke. Well, good people are like the angels in this: they are full of love and compassion, and when they see anyone turning away from sin and doing what is right, it makes them feel happy.

Good people find walking in truth so pleasant that they would like everybody else to walk in truth too. They do not want to keep all this pleasantness to themselves and to go to heaven alone. They want to see everyone around them loving Jesus Christ and obeying Him – all their relatives, all their neighbors, all their old friends, and all their young friends – indeed, all the world. The more people they see walking in truth, the more they are pleased.

Children, John was a good man, and he was full of love to souls – and this was one reason why he rejoiced.

2. John rejoiced because it is very uncommon to see children walking in truth.
Dear children, I am very sorry to tell you that there are many bad boys and girls in the world. Too many are careless, thoughtless, self-willed, and disobedient. Nobody can rejoice over them. I hear many fathers and mothers complaining about this. I hear many schoolteachers speak of it. I am afraid it is quite true.

There are many children who will not give their minds to anything that is good. They will not do what they are told. They like to be idle and to have their own way. They love playing more than learning. They do things that God says are wicked and wrong, and are not ashamed of it. This is all very sad to see.

You can be sure that John had learned this, for he was an elderly man, as well as an apostle, and he had seen many things. He knew that even the children of good people sometimes turn out very badly. I dare say he remembered Jacob and David and all the sorrow their children caused them. No doubt he knew what Solomon says in the book of Proverbs: *Foolishness is bound in the heart of a child* (Proverbs 22:15).

When, therefore, John saw this lady's children not turning out bad like others, but walking in the way that they should go, he might well feel that it was a special mercy. I do not at all wonder that he greatly rejoiced.

3. John rejoiced because he knew that walking in truth would make these children truly happy in this life.
John was not one of those foolish people who do not like a lot of Christianity and imagine that it makes people unhappy. John knew that the more true religion people have, the happier they are.

John knew that life is always full of care and trouble and that the only way to get through life comfortably is to be a real follower and servant of Jesus Christ.

Dear children, remember what I say now: If you ever want to be happy in this evil world, you must give your heart to Jesus Christ and follow Him. Give Him the entire command of your soul and ask Him to be your Savior and your God. Then you will be happy. Have no will of your own, but only try to please Him, and then your life will be pleasant.

Surrender all to Christ, and He will undertake to manage all that concerns your soul. Trust in Him at all times. Trust in Him in every condition – in sickness and in health, in youth and in old age, in poverty and in plenty, in sorrow and in joy. Trust in Him, and He will be a Shepherd to watch over you, a Guide to lead you, a King to protect you, and a Friend to help you in time of need.

Trust in Him, for He Himself says, *I will never leave you nor forsake you* (Hebrews 13:8). He will put His Spirit in you and will give you a new heart. He will give you power to become a true child of God. He will give you grace to keep down your tempers, to no longer be selfish, and to love others as yourself. He will make your cares lighter and your work easier. He will comfort you in times of trouble. Christ can make those people happy who trust in Him. Christ died to save them, and Christ ever lives to give them peace.

Dear children, John was well aware of these things. He had learned them by experience. He saw this lady's children likely to be happy in this world, so it is no wonder that he rejoiced.

4. John rejoiced because he knew that walking in truth in the present life would lead to glory and honor in the life to come.
The life to come is the life we should all think most about. Many people only seem to care about what happens to them in this life, but they are sadly mistaken. This life is very short. It will soon be over. The oldest person you know will tell you that it seems as if only a few years ago he was a child. The life to come is the life of real importance. It will have no end. It will be either never-ending happiness or never-ending pain. Oh, what a serious thought that is!

Children, I do not doubt that John was thinking of the life to come when he rejoiced. Our Lord Jesus Christ had often told him of the glorious rewards prepared for those who walk in truth. John thought of the rewards laid up in heaven for these children, and he was glad.

I do not doubt that John looked forward in his heart to that day when Jesus will come again. I dare say that he saw in his mind's eye these dear children clothed in robes as white as snow, having golden crowns on their heads, standing at Jesus Christ's right hand, and enjoying pleasures forevermore (Psalm 16:11). He saw them and their beloved mother meeting again in heaven – meeting in that blessed place where parting and sorrow will be known no more.

Dear children, these must have been sweet and pleasant thoughts. I do not wonder that John rejoiced.

* * * *

Now I have finished what I had to say about our verse. I have done what I promised. I have told you what it means to walk in truth; that is one important thing. I have told you why John rejoiced so much to find this lady's children walking in truth; that is the other important thing. Let me now wind it all up by saying something that, with God's help, might fasten this lesson in your minds. Sadly, how many lessons are forgotten! I want this lesson to stick in your hearts and do good.

Ask yourselves then, "If John knew me at this time, would he rejoice over me? Would John be pleased if he saw my ways and my behavior, or would he look sorrowful?"

O children, do not neglect this question. This is no light matter. It may be your life. No wise person will ever rejoice over bad children. They may be clean and pretty, have fine clothes, and look good outwardly, but a wise person will feel sad when he sees them if he feels they are wrong inwardly. If they do not have new hearts, they are not going to heaven!

Believe me – it is much better to be good than to be good-looking. It is much better to have grace in your hearts than to have much money in your pockets or fine clothes on your backs. None except children who love Christ are the children who cause a wise person's heart to rejoice.

Beloved children, hear the last words I have to say to you. I give you an invitation from Christ, my Master. I say to you in His name, "Come and walk in truth!"

This is the way to gladden the hearts of your parents and relatives. This is the one thing above all others that will please your ministers and teachers. You do not know how happy you make us when you try to walk in truth. When you are walking in truth, we feel that all is well, even if we die and leave you behind us in this evil world. We feel that your souls are safe, even if we are called away and cannot help you and teach you anymore. We feel that you are on the right way to happiness and that you are prepared for difficulties, no matter how many may come upon you. We know that walking in truth gives peace now, and we are sure that it leads to heaven hereafter.

Come, then, and begin to walk in truth right now. The devil will try to make you think it is too hard – that you cannot do it. Do not believe him; he is a liar! He wants to do you harm. Simply trust in Christ and follow Him, and you will soon say that His way is a way of pleasantness and a path of peace (Proverbs 3:17). Pray for the Holy Spirit to come into your heart, and you will soon feel strong. He can guide you into all truth (John 16:13). Read the Bible regularly, and you will soon be made wise unto salvation (2 Timothy 3:15). The Bible is the word of truth. Read and pray. Pray and read. Begin these habits, and keep them up. Do these things, and before long you will not say that it is impossible to walk in truth. But come – come at once!

Children, in the third chapter of Revelation, I find Jesus Christ saying, *Behold, I stand at the door and knock.* Has this been going on with you? Has Jesus been knocking at the door of your heart all through this lesson? If so, do not keep Him waiting any longer. If so, go to Him now on your knees in prayer. Go to Him at once and ask Him to come in. Ask Jesus to come and dwell in your heart and take care of it as His own. Ask Him to enable you to walk in truth.

Oh, think how many children in the world have never been invited as you are being invited! Think how many boys and girls have never had the chance of being saved that you now have. Think how many would possibly leap for joy and walk in truth at once if they were invited.

Beloved children, take care. You cannot say that you were not invited. Jesus invites you. The Bible invites you. I, the servant of Christ, invite you now. Oh, come to Christ! Come, and be happy. Come, and walk in truth!

Chapter 3

Little and Wise

There be four things which are little upon the earth, but they are exceeding wise: the ants are a people not strong, yet they prepare their meat in the summer; the conies are but a feeble folk, yet make they their houses in the rocks; the locusts have no king, yet go they forth all of them by bands; the spider taketh hold with her hands, and is in kings' palaces.
– Proverbs 30:24-28

Dear children, I would like you all to be very wise. Wisdom is far better than money, fine clothes, large houses, or fancy transportation. People who are not wise seldom get on well in life. They are seldom happy. My best wish for any dear boys and girls that I love is that they will grow up very wise.

"But how are we to be wise?" some of you will ask. "What are we to do in order to get this wisdom that you tell us is such a good thing?"

Dear children, if you want to be wise, you must pray to God to make you so. You must ask Him to put His Holy Spirit in your heart and give you wisdom.

Besides this, you must read God's holy book, the Bible. There you will find out what true wisdom is. There you will see what kind of things wise people do.

Now let me talk to you about the verses in the Bible that are written above. They are verses that tell us about wisdom. I hope they will do you much good.

In these verses, you see that God tells you to learn a lesson from four little creatures: the ant, the cony, the locust, and the spider. He seems to say that they are all patterns of wisdom. They are all poor little weak things. An ant is a little creeping insect that everybody knows. A cony is a little creature very much like a rabbit. A locust is like a large grasshopper. A spider is a thing that the least child does not need to be afraid of. But God tells you that the ant, the cony, the locust, and the spider are very wise. Come then, dear children, and listen to me while I tell you something about them. Some of you are only little now, but you see here that it is possible to be little, yet wise.

First of all, what are you to learn from the ants? You must learn from the little ants to take thought to prepare for the times to come.

The Bible says that the ants are not strong, *yet they provide their food in the summer.* God has made the ants so wise and thoughtful that they go about gathering food in the harvest time. They are not idle in the fine, long days when the sun shines. They get all the grains of corn they can find, and they store them up in their nests. Then when frost and snow come, the ants do not starve. They lay snug in their nests and have plenty to eat.

The butterflies are much prettier to look at than the ants. They have beautiful wings and make a much finer show. But the butterflies, poor things, are not as wise as the ants. They fly about among the flowers and enjoy themselves all summer. They never think of gathering food for the winter. But what happens when the winter comes? The poor butterflies all die, while the ants stay alive.

Now, dear children, I want you to learn wisdom from the ants. I want you, like them, to think of the time to come. You have got within you a soul that will live forever. Your body will die some time, but your soul never will. Your soul needs thought and care as much as your body. It needs to have its sins forgiven. It needs grace to make it please God. It needs power to be good. It needs to have God for its best friend in order to be happy.

Dear children, the best time for seeking forgiveness, grace, and the friendship of God is the time of youth. Youth and childhood are your summer. Now you are strong and well. Now you have plenty of time. Now you have few cares and troubles to distract you. Now is the best time for laying up food for your souls.

My beloved children, you must remember that winter is before you! Old age is your winter. Your frost, snow, rain, and storms are all yet to come. Sorrow, pain, sickness, death, and judgment will all come with old age. Happy are those who get ready for it early. Happy are those who, like the ants, take thought for things to come!

Wise boys and girls read their Bibles and learn many verses by heart. Wise boys and girls pray to God every day to give them His Holy Spirit. Those who are wise obey what their parents and teachers tell them, and they strive to be good. Those who are wise dislike all bad ways and bad words, and they always tell the truth. Such boys and girls are like the little ants. They are laying up supplies against the time to come.

Dear children, if you have not done so before,

I hope you will begin to do so now. If you have done so, I hope you will keep on doing so, and will do so more and more. Do not be like the foolish butterflies. Be like the ants. Think of the time to come – and be wise.

Let us now see what you are to learn from the conies. You must learn from the little conies to have a place of safety to flee to in time of danger.

The Bible says that the conies make their houses in the rocks. The conies are afraid of foxes, dogs, and cruel men who hunt and kill them. They are poor weak things, and they are not strong enough to fight and take care of themselves. So what do they do? They make their holes among stones and rocks whenever they can. They go where people cannot dig them out. They go where dogs and foxes cannot follow them. Then, when they see people, dogs, or foxes coming, they run away into those holes and are safe.

The wolf can run much faster than the cony, for it has much longer legs. The deer is much bigger than the cony, and has got fine antlers. But the wolf and the deer do not have holes to run into. They lie out on the open fields. When people come to hunt them with dogs and guns, they are soon caught and killed. But the little cony has a hiding place to run to, and in this way it often escapes.

Dear children, I want you to learn wisdom from the little conies. I want you to have a place of safety for your souls.

Your soul has many enemies. You are in danger from many things that may do them harm. You each have a wicked heart within you. Have you not often found how hard it is to be good? You each have a terrible enemy who is seeking to ruin you forever and take you to hell. That enemy is the devil. You cannot see him, but he is never far away. You live in a world where there are many bad people and few good people. Dear children, all these things are against you.

You need the help of One who can keep you safe! You need a hiding place for your precious soul. You need a dear Friend who is able to save you from your evil hearts, from the devil, and from the bad example of wicked people. Listen to me, and I will tell you about Him.

There is One who is able to keep your soul quite safe. His name is Jesus Christ. He is strong enough to save you, for He is God's own Son. He is willing to save you, for He came down from heaven and died upon the cross for sinners. When He was on earth, He took children up in His arms and blessed them (Mark 10:16).

Dear children, those boys and girls are wise who put their trust in Jesus Christ and ask Him to take care of their souls. Such boys and girls will be kept safe. Jesus Christ loves them. Jesus Christ will not let them come to harm. He will not allow the devil or wicked people to ruin their souls. Jesus is the true rock for children to flee to. Boys and girls who trust Him will be cared for while they live and will go to heaven when they die. Jesus is the only true hiding place. Boys and girls who love Him will be safe and happy.

Dear children, I hope you will try to have your soul kept safe. Do not put off asking the Lord Jesus Christ to take care of it. Do not say to yourself, "Oh, I will have plenty of time. I will do this later!" Who knows what may happen to you before long? Maybe you will be sick and ill. Maybe you will lose all your kind friends and will be left alone. Oh, go and pray to Jesus now! Be like the wise little conies. Get a safe hiding place for your soul.

Let us now see what you are to learn from the locusts. You must learn from the locusts to love one another, to keep together, and to help one another.

The Bible says that the locusts have no king, yet they go forth together in ranks. They have nobody over them to tell them what to do. They are poor little weak insects by themselves. One locust alone can do very little. The smallest boy or girl would kill a locust if he were to step on it. It would be dead at once.

However, the little locusts are so wise that they always stay together. They fly about in such numbers that you could not count them. You would think they were a black cloud. They do not quarrel with one another. They help each other. In this way, the locusts are able to do a very great deal. They make the farmers and gardeners quite afraid when they are seen coming. They eat up the grass and grain. They strip all the leaves off the trees. This is because they help one another.

Dear children, I want you to learn from the little locusts to always love one another and to never quarrel. You should try to be kind and helpful to other boys and girls. You should make it a rule never to be selfish, never to be mean, never to get angry, and never to fight with one another. Boys and girls who are selfish and who quarrel and fight are not wise. They are more foolish than the locusts!

Dear children, quarreling is very wicked. It pleases the devil, for he is always trying to make people wicked like himself. It does not please God, for God is love. Selfishness and quarreling are most improper in Christian children. They should try to be like Christ. Christ was never selfish. He did not try to please Himself, but others.

Think what a great deal of good boys and girls

could do if they would be like the little locusts and love one another. Think how useful they might be to their fathers and mothers. They could save them much trouble and help in many little ways. Think what a great deal of money they could collect to help the missionaries go to the poor heathen. If every child in this country were to collect ten dollars a year to help the missionaries, it would be a very large amount. Above all, think what good boys and girls might do if they agree to pray for one another. How happy they would soon be! Such prayers would be heard.

Dear children, as long as you live, love one another. Try to be of one mind. Do not have anything to do with quarreling and fighting. Hate it and think of it as a great sin. You should agree together far better than the little locusts. They have no king to teach them. You have a King who has promised His Spirit to teach you – and that King is Christ! Oh, be wise like the locusts – and love one another!

Last, let us see what you are to learn from the spider. You must learn from the spider not to give up trying to be good because of a little trouble.

The Bible says that the spider can be caught with the hand, yet it is found in kings' palaces. The spider is a poor little feeble thing, but the spider takes much effort in making her web. The spider creeps into expensive houses and climbs to the top of the finest rooms, and there she spins her web. There seems to be no way to keep her out. Your mother comes and brushes the web away. The spider sets to work at once and makes a new web. No little creature is as persevering as the spider. She does her work over and over again. She will not give up!

I remember a story of a great king who got his kingdom back by following the example from a spider. Poor man! He had been driven away from his kingdom, like David, by wicked rebels. He had often tried to get his kingdom back. He had fought many battles, but had always been beaten. At last he began to think it was no use. He would give up and fight no more.

It just so happened at that time that he was lying awake in bed very early one summer's morning when he saw a spider at work. The spider was trying to make a thread from one side of the room to the other. Twelve times she tried in vain. Twelve times the thread broke. Twelve times the spider fell to the ground. Twelve times she got up and tried again. She did not give up. She persevered, and the thirteenth time she succeeded!

When the king saw that, he said to himself, "Why should I not persevere, too, in trying to get back my kingdom? Why should I not succeed at last, even though I have so often failed?" He tried again, and he succeeded. He conquered his cruel enemies and got his kingdom back. Dear children, this king's name was Robert Bruce. He got back his kingdom in Scotland by copying the spider!

Now I want you to make the spider your pattern about your soul. I want you, like the spider, to persevere in sticking to what is good. I would like you to determine that you will never give up. I want you to keep on trying not to do what is evil, and always trying to do what is good and pleasing to God.

Dear children, I am sorry to say that it is a wicked world and that there are many people who will try hard to make you wicked as you grow up. The devil will try hard to make you forget God. Bad men and women will tell you there is no need for you to be so good.

I beg you not to give in to them. I urge you to persevere. Keep on praying every day. Keep on reading your Bibles regularly. Keep on regularly going to church on Sunday. Sadly, there are many boys and girls who give up everything that is good as soon as they leave school. While they are at school they use their Bibles and devotional books, but when they leave school they stop using all their good books. They often get into bad company, take up bad ways, and forget to honor God on the Lord's Day. They seem to forget all that has been taught to them. This is not persevering. This is being more foolish than the little spider! It is wicked and unwise!

Dear children, there is a glorious house in heaven where I hope I will see some of you. There is a palace there, belonging to Jesus Christ, that is far finer than any palace on earth, in which all Jesus Christ's people will live and be happy forever and ever. Dear children, I hope I will see many of you there.

Remember, though, that if you and I are to meet in this glorious palace, you must persevere and take effort regarding your souls. You must pray earnestly. You must read your Bibles regularly. You must fight against sin daily. When bad people entice you to do wrong, you must say, "I will not give up my belief in Jesus Christ! I will try to please Christ." Oh, let the little spider be your pattern all your lives! Persevere and be wise.

Now, dear children, I will finish by asking you to think about what I have been telling you. I have told you about four little creatures that are very wise: the ants, the conies, the locusts, and the spiders. I have shown you that the ants are a pattern of wisdom because they think about time to come. The conies are a pattern of wisdom because they make their houses in safe places. The locusts are a pattern of wisdom because they help one another. The spiders are a pattern of wisdom because they persevere.

Dear children, I want you to be like them. Some of you may possibly never live to be men and women, but there is one thing you can be even now: you can be wise.

Be wise like the ants. Consider these two verses of the Bible and learn them by heart: *Remember now thy Creator in the days of thy youth* (Ecclesiastes 12:1). *Prepare to meet thy God* (Amos 4:12).

Be wise like the conies. Consider these two verses of the Bible and learn them by heart: *Believe on the Lord Jesus Christ, and thou shalt be saved* (Acts 16:31). *Thou art my hiding place; thou shalt preserve me from trouble* (Psalm 32:7).

Be wise like the locusts. Consider these two verses of the Bible and learn them by heart: *By this shall all men know that ye are my disciples, if ye have love one to another* (John 13:35). *He that loveth not his brother whom he hath seen, how can he love God whom he hath not seen?* (1 John 4:20).

Be wise like the spiders. Consider these words of the Bible and learn them by heart: *Ask, and it shall be given you; seek, and ye shall find* (Matthew 7:7). *Let us lay aside every weight, and the sin which doth so easily beset us, and let us run with patience the race that is set before us, looking unto Jesus the author and finisher of our faith* (Hebrews 12:1-2).

Dear children, think about these things. This is the way to be both happy and wise. Never forget what God says in the Bible: *Better is a poor and a wise child than an old and foolish king* (Ecclesiastes 4:13). *The wise shall inherit glory* (Proverbs 3:35).

Chapter 4

No More Crying!

God shall wipe away all tears from their eyes; and there shall be no more death, neither sorrow, nor crying, neither shall there be any more pain.
– Revelation 21:4

Beloved children, I would like you to read the Bible verse above. Then read it again. I am going to tell you something that I hope will make you remember that verse as long as you live.

I am going to tell you about three places of which the Bible says a great deal. It matters little what we know about some places, but it matters much to know something about the three places of which I am now going to speak.

- First, there is a place where there is a great deal of crying.

- Second, there is a place where there is nothing else but crying.

- Third, there is a place where there is no crying at all.

Now listen to me, and I will tell you a few things worth knowing.

First of all, there is a place where there is a great deal of crying.
What is that place? It is the world in which we live. It is a world full of beautiful and pleasant things. The sun shining by day and the stars by night; the green hills looking up to heaven; the rolling sea ebbing and flowing; the broad, quiet lakes; the rushing restless rivers; the flowers blooming in the spring; the fields full of grain in autumn; the birds singing in the woods; and the lambs playing in the meadows – these are all beautiful things! I could look at them for hours and say, "What a beautiful world it is!" Still, however, it is a world where there is a great deal of crying. It is a world where there are many tears.

There was crying in Bible times. Hagar wept when she thought Ishmael was dying. Abraham mourned when Sarah died. Joseph wept when his brothers sold him into Egypt. David wept when Absalom was killed. There was weeping at Jerusalem when good king Josiah was slain in battle. There was weeping at Bethlehem when Herod killed all the little children who were under two years old. You will find these things, and many like them, in your Bibles.

There is crying now all over the world. Little babies cry when they want anything or when they feel pain. Boys and girls cry when they are hurt, frightened, or corrected. Grown-up people sometimes cry when they are in trouble or when they see those whom they love die. Wherever there is sorrow and pain, there is crying.

I dare say you have seen people come to church all dressed in black. That is called being in mourning. Some relative or friend of these people has died, and therefore they dress in black. When you see people in mourning, someone has been crying.

I dare say you have seen graves in cemeteries, and you have heard that when people die, they are buried there. Some of them are very little graves – shorter than you are. When those graves were made and little coffins were lowered down into them, there was crying.

Children, did you ever think about where all this crying came from? Did you ever consider how crying first began? Did you ever hear how weeping and tears came into the world? God did not make crying – that is certain. All that God made was *very good* (Genesis 1:31). Listen to me, and I will tell you how crying began.

Crying came into the world by reason of sin. Sin is the cause of all the weeping, tears, sorrow, and pain that are upon earth. All the crying began when Adam and Eve ate the forbidden fruit and became sinners. It was sin that brought pain, sickness, and death into the world. It was sin that brought selfishness, lying, unkindness, quarreling, stealing, and fighting into the world. If there had been no wickedness, there would have been no weeping. If there had been no sin, there would have been no crying.

See now, my beloved children, how much you should hate sin! All the unhappiness in the world came from sin. How strange and astonishing it is that anyone can take pleasure in sin! Do not let that be the case with you. Be on guard against sin. Fight with it. Avoid it. Do not listen to it. Take the advice of the apostle Paul: *Abhor that which is evil* (Romans 12:9). Take the advice of King Solomon: *If sinners entice thee, consent thou not* (Proverbs 1:10). Say to yourself every morning, "Sin caused crying, so I will hate sin!"

See, again, my beloved children, how foolish it

is to expect perfect happiness in this world. It is expecting what you will not find. This world is a place where there is much crying and where things do not always go on pleasantly. I hear many boys and girls talking of pleasures they will have when they are grown men and women. I feel sorry for them when I hear them talking in this way. I know they are mistaken. I know they will be disappointed. They will find that when they grow up they cannot get through the world without many troubles and cares. There are no roses without thorns. There are no years without dark and rainy days. There is no living on earth without crying and tears!

I will now speak of the second place about which I promised to tell you something.

Second, there is a place where there is nothing else but crying.
What is this place? It is the place to which all bad people go when they are dead. It is the place that the Bible calls hell. In hell, there is no laughter or smiling. There is nothing but weeping and wailing and gnashing of teeth (Matthew 13:42; Luke 13:28)! In hell, there is no happiness. Those who go there cry all day and all night without stopping. They have no rest. They never go to sleep happy or wake up happy. They never stop crying in hell.

Beloved children, I am sorry to tell you that there

are many people going to hell. *Wide is the gate, and broad is the way, that leadeth to destruction, and many there be which go in thereat* (Matthew 7:13). I am afraid that many children are going to hell. I see many boys and girls who are so disobedient and poorly behaved that I am sure they are not prepared for heaven. If they are not ready for heaven, where will they go if they die? There is only one other place to which they can go. They will go to hell!

Dear children, it makes me sad to say these things. I cannot bear the thought of boys and girls going to that dreadful place where there is nothing but crying. My heart's desire and prayer to God for you is that you will not go to hell. But I want you to know some things that you must pay attention to if you would not go to hell. Listen to me now while I ask you a few questions.

Do you love Jesus Christ? You should love Him. He died upon the cross for sins so that He could save people from hell. He allowed Himself to be closed up in the dark prison of the grave so sins could be forgiven and so people would not need to be chained in hell forever. Dear children, think about this! If you love nothing except playing, eating sweets, nice clothes, and storybooks – but do not love Christ, you are not in the right way! Take care! When bad people die, they will go to hell – the place where there is nothing but crying.

Do you try to please Christ? You should do so. I read in the Bible that Jesus Christ said, *If ye love me, keep my commandments* (John 14:15). He also said, *Ye are my friends, if ye do whatsoever I command you* (John 15:14). Dear children, think about this! If you are selfish or angry or tell lies or quarrel with one another or do not obey as you are told – you are not Christ's friends. Take care! When you die, you will go to hell – the place where there is nothing but crying.

Do you pray? You should do so. God will never be a friend to you if you do not speak to Him and ask Him to take care of your soul and make you good. If you never pray, or if you say your prayers without thinking, your heart will soon be full of mischief and sin. It will never stay empty for a day. I once heard of a boy who was given a little garden full of flowers. However, he did nothing to take care of it. He never raked it or weeded it. After a few weeks, the weeds came up so thick that the flowers died. Dear children, think of this! If you do not ask God to put the Holy Spirit in your hearts, the devil will soon fill them with sin! Take care! When you die, you will go to hell – the place where there is nothing but crying.

Do you read your Bible? You should do so. That beautiful book is able to keep you from hell and save your soul. If you use the Bible properly, you will not be hurt by the devil. I once heard of a little boy in Africa who was sleeping beside his father in the open air near a fire. He awoke in the middle of the night and saw a large lion close to him looking as if he was going to seize him. The little boy picked up a burning stick out of the fire and put it in the lion's face – and drove the lion away.

Dear children, think of this! The devil is *a roaring lion . . . seeking whom he may devour* (1 Peter 5:8). But he cannot harm you if you make a right use of the Bible. If you want to drive him from you, you must read your Bible. If you can read, yet you neglect your Bible, you are in great danger. Take care! When you die, you will go to hell – the place where there is nothing but crying.

Beloved children, remember my four questions. Think of them often, and test your own hearts by them. I am not afraid for children who love Jesus and try to please Him, and who pray and read their Bibles. I am not afraid that they will go to hell if they die. But I am afraid for children who care nothing about these things. I think they are in great danger of going to hell!

I will now speak of the third place about which I promised to tell you something.

*Third, there is a place where
there is no crying at all.*
What is this place? It is heaven. It is the place to which all godly people go when they die. In heaven, all is joy and happiness. No tears are shed there. Sorrow and pain and sickness and death can never enter in there. There can be no crying in heaven because there is nothing there that can cause grief.

There will be no more work in heaven. People will no longer need to labor for their food. The head will no longer have to ache with thinking. The hands will no longer be painful with hard work. There will be an eternal rest for all the people of God.

There will be no sickness in heaven. Pain and disease and weakness and death will not be known. The people who dwell there will never say, "I am sick." They will always be well. There will be nothing but health and strength forevermore.

There will be no sin in heaven. There will be no angry tempers, no unkind words, and no spiteful actions. The great tempter, the devil, will not be allowed to come in and spoil the happiness. There will be nothing but holiness and love forevermore.

Best of all, the Lord Jesus Christ Himself will be in the midst of heaven. His people will at last see Him face to face and will never leave His presence! He will gather His lambs into His arms and will wipe away all tears from all eyes. Where Jesus is will be fullness of joy, and at His right hand will be pleasures forevermore.

Dear children, wouldn't you like to go to heaven? We cannot live forever in this world. A day will come when we must die, like so many others who have died already. Children, wouldn't you like to go to heaven when you die? Listen to me, and I will tell you something about the way by which you must go to heaven.

If you want to go to heaven, you must have your sins forgiven and your hearts made new and good. There is only one being who can do this for you. That one is the Lord Jesus Christ. God has appointed Him to be the friend of sinners. He can wash away your sins in His own precious blood. He can make your hearts new by putting the Holy Spirit in them. Jesus is the Way and the Door into heaven. He has the key to heaven in His hand. Children, if you want to go to heaven, you must ask Jesus Christ to let you in.

Ask Jesus in prayer to prepare a place for you in that world where there is no crying. Ask Him to put your name in His book of life and to make you one of His people. Ask Him to cleanse you from all your sins and to put the Holy Spirit in your heart. Ask Him to give you power to fight His battle against sin, the world, and the devil. Ask Him to give you grace to make you good while you are young, and good when you grow up, so that you may be safe while you live and happy forever when you die.

Children, Jesus Christ is ready to do all this if you will only ask Him. He has done it for many people already. He is waiting to do it for you at this very moment. Do not be afraid to ask Him. Tell Him that you have heard that He was very kind to people when He was on earth, and ask Him to be kind to you. Remind Him how kind He was to the poor dying thief on the cross. Say to Him, "Lord Jesus, remember me; I want to go to heaven. Lord, think upon me. Lord, give me the Holy Spirit. Lord, forgive my sins and give me a new heart. Lord Jesus, save me!"

Well, children, I have kept my word. I have told you about three places. I have told you about a place where there is nothing but crying. I hope none of you will go there. I have told you about a place where there is no crying. I hope you will all go there. I have told you about a place where there is much crying. That place is the world in which you are living. Would you like now to know the best way to be happy in this world? Listen to me, and I will tell you.

The happiest people in this world are those who make the Bible the guide and standard of their lives. They read their Bibles often. They believe what the Bible says. They love the Savior Jesus Christ of whom the Bible speaks. They try to obey what the Bible commands. None are as happy as these people. They cannot prevent sickness and trouble from sometimes coming to them, but they learn from the Bible to bear them patiently. Children, if you want to get through the world happily, make the Bible your best friend.

I will tell you a story that I once heard about a little boy and the Bible. It might help you to remember what I have just been saying. I want the words I have just written to stick forever in your minds.

"Father," said this little boy one day, "I do not see any use in reading the Bible. I do not see that it does people any good." Little Johnny said this in a rather grouchy and cranky way, and his father thought it best not to begin reasoning with him.

"Johnny," he said, "put on your hat and go for a walk with me."

Johnny's father first took him to a house where there was an old woman who was very poor, and he talked to her about her poverty. "Sir," said the old woman, "I do not complain. I have read in the Bible these words from Philippians 4:11: *I have learned, in whatever state I am, therewith to be content.*"

"Johnny," said the little boy's father, "hear what the old woman says."

They went on to another house where there was a young woman who was very ill and who was never likely to get better. Johnny's father asked her if she felt afraid to die. "No!" she said. "I find it written in the Bible, in Psalm 23:4, *Though I walk through the valley of the shadow of death, I will fear no evil, for thou art with me.*"

"Johnny," said the little boy's father again, "hear what the young woman says."

Children, when Johnny and his father got home that afternoon from their walk, his father asked him one question: "Johnny," he said, "do you think it is of any use to read the Bible? Do you think reading the Bible does people any good?"

What do you think Johnny said? I will tell you. He held down his head and said nothing, but his face got very red and he looked very much ashamed. Children, from that very day Johnny was never heard again to say, "It is of no use reading the Bible."

Beloved children, remember my parting words. The way to get through the world with the least possible crying is to read the Bible, believe the Bible, pray over the Bible, and live by the Bible.

The person who goes through life in this way will have the least crying in this world, and best of all, he will have no crying at all in the world to come.

Chapter 5

The Happy Little Girl

Dear children, would you like to know who was the happiest child I ever saw? Listen to me, and I will tell you.

The happiest child I ever saw was a little girl whom I once met traveling in a railway carriage. We were both going on a journey to London, and we traveled a great many miles together. She was only eight years old, and she was blind. She had never been able to see at all. She had never seen the sun, the stars, the sky, the grass, the flowers, the trees, the birds, and all those pleasant things that you see every day of your lives; but still she was quite happy.

She was by herself, poor little thing. She had no friends or relatives to take care of her on the journey and to be good to her, but she was quite happy and content. When she got into the carriage, she said, "Tell me how many people there are in the carriage. I am blind, and I can see nothing."

A gentleman asked her if she was afraid. "No," she said, "I am not frightened. I have traveled before, and I trust in God – and people are always very good to me."

I soon learned the reason why she was so happy, and what do you think it was? She loved Jesus Christ, and Jesus Christ loved her. She had sought Jesus Christ, and she had found Him.

I began to talk to her about the Bible, and I soon saw that she knew a great deal of it. She went to a school where the teacher used to read the Bible to her, and she was a good girl and had remembered what her teacher had read.

Dear children, you cannot imagine how many things in the Bible this poor little blind girl knew. I only wish that every grown-up person in this country knew as much as she did. I will try and tell you some of what she knew about the Bible.

She talked to me about sin. She talked about how sin first came into the world when Adam and Eve ate the forbidden fruit, and how it was to be seen everywhere now. "Oh," she said, "there are no really good people! The very best people in the world have many sins every day, and I am sure we all waste a great deal of time, even if we do nothing else wrong. We are all such sinners! There is nobody who has not sinned a great many sins."

Then she talked about Jesus Christ. She told me about the agony in the garden of Gethsemane. She talked about His sweating drops of blood, about the soldiers nailing Him to the cross, about the spear piercing His side, and about blood and water coming out. "Oh," she said, "how very good it was of Him to die for us, and such a cruel death! How good He was to suffer so for our sins."

Then she talked about wicked people. She told me she was afraid that there were a great many wicked people in the world, and it made her very unhappy to see how many of her fellow school members and acquaintances lived. "But," she said, "I know the reason why they are so wicked: it is because they do not try to be good; they do not want to be good; they do not ask Jesus to make them good."

I asked her what part of the Bible she liked best. She told me she liked all the history of Jesus Christ, but the chapters she liked the most were the three last chapters of the book of Revelation. I had a Bible with me, and I took it out and read these chapters to her as we went along.

When I was done, she began to talk about heaven. "Think," she said, "how nice it will be to be there! There will be no more sorrow, nor crying, nor tears. And Jesus Christ will be there, for it says, *the Lamb is the light thereof,* and we will always be with Him! Also, there will be no night there. They will need no candle nor light of the sun."

Dear children, just think of this poor little blind girl. Think of her taking pleasure in talking about Jesus Christ. Think of her rejoicing in the account of heaven, where there will be no sorrow nor night.

I have not seen that girl since. She went to her own home in London, and I do not know whether she is alive or not; but I hope she is, and I have no doubt Jesus Christ has taken good care of her.

Dear children, are you as happy and as cheerful as she was?

You are not blind. You have eyes, and you can run around and see everything. You can go where you like, and you can read to yourselves as much as you please. But are you as happy as this poor little girl?

Oh, if you want to be happy in this world, remember my advice today. Do as the little blind girl did. Love Jesus Christ, and He will love you. Seek Him early, and you will find Him.

Chapter 6

Seeking the Lord Early

I love them that love me; and those that seek me early shall find me. – Proverbs 8:17

Children, I am going to talk to you about Jesus Christ and your souls. I want to make you happy, but I know that people are never really happy unless their souls are happy – and I am sure that people's souls cannot be happy unless they love Jesus Christ. That is the reason I am going to write to you now. I want to tell you something about Jesus Christ and your souls.

Dear children, I hope you will all pay close attention. I pray that the Spirit of God will come into your hearts and make you able to do so. Try to listen to me. Try to understand what I say. Try to remember and carry away something in your minds. I hope to do you all a great deal of good. Do not forget I am writing to you – not to the grown-up people – but to you, only to you.

Now just think what a pleasant verse we have here: *I love them that love me; and those that seek me early shall find me.*

These are sweet words indeed. Who do you think says them? They are said by the Lord Jesus Christ, the Son of God, the Savior of the world. He is called "Wisdom" in this chapter. We know it means Jesus Christ, for there are things said about Wisdom in this chapter that cannot be truly said about anyone except Jesus Christ Himself.

Come, now, and let us see what Jesus Christ says. Listen, dear children, for this is very important.

I. He tells us, *I love them that love me.* Now what can we make of this?

First of all, do you not think that it is very pleasant to hear that there are people whom Jesus Christ loves? We all like to be loved in this world. Think how disagreeable it would be for you and me if there were nobody alive who loved us. Suppose that no man or woman cared at all for us. Suppose that everybody neglected us and left us alone. What would we do? We would be wretched, miserable, and unhappy! I am sure we all like to be loved.

Well, then, just consider what a blessed thing

it must be to be loved by Jesus Christ – by the Son of God Himself!

You know that sometimes people love us in this world, yet can do nothing for us. Your dear fathers and mothers love you, but maybe they are poor and cannot buy what you need; or maybe they are sick and very old and are not able to help you.

But, dear children, these are things that can never happen to Jesus Christ, and I will tell you why.

Jesus Christ is very great. He is King of Kings and Lord of Lords. He is Maker of all things. He is Almighty. He is able to do anything that He likes.

Oh, what a thing it must be to be loved by Jesus Christ!

Jesus Christ is very rich. He has got everything to give away that you can need, either for soul or body. He keeps the keys of heaven. He has got an endless store of blessings in His treasure house – far more than I could describe.

Oh, what a thing it must be to be loved by Jesus Christ!

Jesus Christ is very good. He never refuses anyone who asks Him favors in a proper way. He was never known to say, "No!" to anyone who made a prayer to Him with a meek and humble heart.

Oh, what a thing it must be to be loved by Jesus Christ!

Dear children, consider these things. Do you

want a great friend? Do you want a rich friend? Do you want a kind friend? Is this the sort of friend you would like? You can be sure there is no friend in all the world like Jesus Christ. There is no love so well worth having as the love of Jesus Christ.

Blessed and happy are those whom Jesus Christ loves. I could not tell you a tenth part of all the great things He does for their souls.

He pardons all their sins. He forgives all the bad things they do. He washes them in His own blood and makes them whiter than snow so that not a spot of sin remains! Dear children, I think that is just what you and I need. We have all sinned many, many sins.

In addition to this, He gives them power to become good. He puts His Spirit in their hearts and makes them love God's ways and like to walk in them. Dear children, that, too, is just the thing you and I need. We have very bad, wicked hearts by nature. We never love God's ways on our own.

Besides this, He takes care that none whom He loves will be lost. He keeps them as a shepherd keeps his sheep. He will not allow either wicked people or the devil to destroy their souls. Dear children, that, too, is just what you and I need. We are all very weak, foolish creatures. We would never be safe if left to ourselves.

Lastly, Jesus is getting a place in heaven ready

for those whom He loves. He has a glorious house for them there, far away from sin, sorrow, and trouble. Dear children, that, too, is good news for you and me. Is it not pleasant to know that He has prepared a home for us so that whenever we leave this world, we will go to a place of peace and rest?

The Lord Jesus Christ does all these things for those whom He loves. Only look at them! What mighty things, what glorious things they are! He cleanses them from all their sins. He gives them power to be good. He takes care that they are not lost. He prepares a house for them in heaven.

Dear children, this is indeed love. This is love worth having. Did I not tell you truly that there is nothing in all the world to be compared to Christ's love – that there is nothing like being loved by Jesus Christ?

II. Let us see next who those are whom Jesus Christ loves. He tells us in our verse. He says, *I love them that love me.*

How can we know whether we love Jesus Christ or not? This is indeed an important question. Are there no characteristics or signs by which those who love Him may be found out? Yes, dear children, I think there are. I will now try to show you what those characteristics and signs are.

Those who love Jesus Christ believe whatever He says in the Bible.

The Bible says we are all sinners – lost, perishing sinners full of wickedness and deceit, deserving nothing but God's anger and wrath. Many people cannot quite believe this. They cannot bring themselves to think they are so bad. They dislike to be told this. This is not so with those who love Jesus Christ. They believe it all. They are ready to say, "It is true, true, quite true."

The Bible tells us that we must come to Christ and trust only in Him if we are to be saved. It says that nothing but His blood can wash away our sins, that it is only for His sake that anyone can be forgiven. Many people will not believe this either. They cannot imagine that their own goodness will not help get them to heaven. But those who love Jesus Christ believe it all. They take the Lord at His word. They stop trusting in their own goodness and are ready to say, "None but Christ – no one but Christ is my Savior!"

Dear children, no one can love Jesus Christ who does not believe what He says. Think what a sad thing it would be if you and I could not get our relatives to believe us. Only imagine how mean and unkind it would seem if they were to say, "We do not depend at all on what you tell us. We cannot trust your word." I am sure we would suppose that they no longer loved us. This, then, is one characteristic of those who love Jesus Christ. They never doubt what He tells them. They believe every word.

Those who love Jesus Christ try to please Him. You know that when you love people, you try to please them. You try to do what they tell you. You try to behave as they want you to behave. You try to remember what they teach you and to pay attention to what they tell you. And why do you do so? Because you love them.

You not only try to please them before their faces when they can see you, but you also try to please them when they are gone away and are out of sight. True love makes you always think, "What would my dear friends like me to do?" If your father and mother found you doing naughty things, doing what they told you not to do, they might well say, "Child, child, I am afraid you do not really love me!" Yes, indeed they might. True love will always cause true obedience, and the Bible says, *Even a child is known by his doings* (Proverbs 20:11).

Now, dear children, just as you try to please your friends and family members if you love them, so those who love Jesus Christ try to please Him. They are always trying to do His will, to keep His laws, to live according to His commandments, and to obey His precepts. They do not think that any of Christ's commands are burdensome. They never say that His laws are hard, strict, and disagreeable. It is their delight to walk in His paths.

Dear children, no man, woman, or child can really love Jesus Christ if they do not try to obey Him. Jesus said, *Ye are my friends, if ye do whatsoever I command you* (John 15:14). This, then, is another certain characteristic of those who love Jesus Christ. They try to please Him in all things.

We have now got through one part of our verse. Sit still and think for a moment about what you have heard. Ask your own heart this: "Do I love Jesus Christ or not? Do I believe what He says, and do I try to please Him?" Those who can answer "Yes," are the children He especially loves. Remember what He says: *I love them that love me.*

III. Let us look next to the other part of our verse and see what we can learn from it. I really think this part is almost as pleasant as the first, for it contains a sweet promise: *those that seek me early shall find me.*

Dear children, how are we to seek Jesus Christ? He does not live upon earth like one of us. We cannot see Him with our eyes. We cannot reach Him and take hold of Him with our hands. Yet He says, *Those that seek me early shall find me.* What can this mean? Let me try to tell you.

First of all, you must seek Jesus Christ in His

own Book. The Bible is Jesus Christ's book, and all who want to know Him must be very diligent in reading their Bibles. He says to each one of you, *Search the scriptures* (John 5:39). He will give the Holy Spirit to those who seek Him in the Scriptures, and He will teach them all about Himself.

Dear children, be regular readers of the Bible every day. Let the Word of God dwell in you richly, and then you will be truly wise (Colossians 3:16). Read it daily. Read a great deal of it. Try to remember it. Memorize it. I remember a little girl in my first church who could learn seventy verses of the Bible in a week. How pleasant it is to find the apostle Paul reminding Timothy that from a child he had known the Holy Scriptures (2 Timothy 3:15). Why should you not be like Timothy in this? I would like to hear that you were all Bible-reading children – children who read the Bible at home, as well as at school.

This, then, is one way to seek Jesus Christ. You must seek Him in the Bible.

Secondly, you must seek Jesus Christ in His own house. Jesus Christ has many houses in this country where people meet together to pray to Him and to hear about Him. Wherever two or three are gathered together in Jesus Christ's name, the Lord Himself really is present, even though we cannot see Him with our eyes (Matthew 18:20).

Dear children, I hope you will all regularly go to Jesus Christ's house as long as you live. I hope you will never do like those foolish people who stay away from it. Oh, what sad harm they are doing to their poor souls!

When you go, try to obey all you hear and to get good from it. Do not look all around, make noises, or talk to other children – but listen well to all that is read or preached. Jesus Christ is there, and He sees how you behave. He loves to see little children coming to His house and behaving well. If you persevere in doing so, you can be sure that He will put His Spirit in you and fill you with all knowledge.

This, then, is another way to seek Jesus Christ. You must seek Him in His house.

Thirdly, you must seek Jesus Christ on your knees in prayer. You must ask Him with your own mouth to give you everything that your soul needs. You must ask Him to cleanse you from all your sins in His blood. You must ask Him to give you His Spirit. You must ask Him to make you good, obedient, gentle, kind, truth-speaking children and to keep you from being selfish, lazy, greedy, angry, deceitful, or bad-tempered. You must tell Him everything that you are afraid of, everything that you feel, and all that you desire to have for your soul. This is prayer.

You do not need to be afraid of Him at all when you pray. He would like you to tell Him everything in your own simple way – just as you tell your own parents when you need anything. Jesus loves children very much. He was once much displeased with His disciples because they prevented people from bringing their children to Him. He told them to allow the little children to come to Him and not to keep them away (Matthew 19:14). He is just the same now as He was then.

Dear children, I would like you all to be praying children. I would like you all to be children who tell the Lord all your needs and are not afraid to speak to Him. Prayer is the surest way to seek Him, and without prayer, your souls will never prosper.

Do not be concerned if your prayers seem very poor and weak. Only let them come from your heart, and the Lord hears them. The Lord Jesus hears every prayer that is sincerely prayed to Him. The least prayer of a little child on earth is loud enough to be heard plainly in heaven above. Heaven seems to be a long way off, but you can be sure that the very moment the prayer is spoken, it is heard there.

A little key will often open a large door. Prayer is a little key of that kind. It can open the door of heaven and take you up to the very throne of God

Himself. Blessed are they who delight in prayer and call much upon God.

This, then, is the third way to seek the Lord Jesus Christ. You must seek Him in prayer.

Dear children, I have told you how to seek the Lord. Before you go any further, ask yourselves, "Do I really seek Him?"

IV. Our verse tells us something about those who seek Jesus Christ, and what is it? It says that they will find Him.

The Lord promises that those who seek Him will find Him. How sweet it is to hear that! Think how disagreeable it would be to seek and seek all our lives and never find Him. But the Lord says that they will find Him.

Now I want to tell you what this "finding" means. We will not see Him with our eyes, for He is sitting at God's right hand in heaven, and not on earth – yet we are told we will find Him. How can this be? Let me tell you.

You will find the Lord's presence in your own heart and mind. You will feel something within you, as if the Lord Jesus Christ were sitting by you and taking care of you, putting His arm around you, smiling upon you, and speaking kindly to you. Just as a blind person feels brighter and happier when the sun is shining pleasantly on him even though he cannot see it, so you and I, if we seek Jesus Christ sincerely, will soon feel our hearts lighter and happier, and something within us will make us know that we have found Him.

Dear children, it is indeed sweet and comfortable when we feel that we have really found Jesus Christ. Oh, that you may never give up seeking until you have found Him! I know that you will find Him if you continue seeking, for He is not far off (Acts 17:27). He is very near every one of us. He is waiting for us to call upon Him.

When you have found Him, you will feel as if you have a sure friend in whom you can trust. He is a friend who will always love you, always watch over you, always take care of you, and always be good to you. He will never fail you.

When you have found Him, you will feel as if you have strength and power to walk in God's ways, strength to keep yourself from bad words and bad company, and strength to do things that please God.

When you have found Him, you will feel as if you had a pleasant Comforter living in your heart. You will be far more happy, cheerful, and content than you were before. Little things will not upset you as they used to. You will not be afraid of sickness, pain, or death.

Dear children, how delightful it will be to feel all this! Try, do try to find Jesus Christ.

V. Now there is only one more thing in our verse that I want to talk to you about. It is only one little word, but that little word is so very important that I dare not pass over it. It is the word "early." *Those that seek me early,* **the Lord Jesus Christ says. They are the ones who will find Him.**

Dear children, that word "early" was meant specifically for you. Seeking Jesus Christ early means seeking Jesus Christ when you are quite young, and that is just what I want you to do.

Children, the Lord sends a message to you this very day. He would like you to begin seeking Him at once. Remember that you cannot begin seeking Jesus too soon.

Seeking early is the safest way. Children may be young and healthy, but no child is too young and healthy to die. Death is very strong, and it can soon make the healthiest of you wither away and make your rosy cheeks pale and sickly. Death is very cruel. It does not mind whom he takes away out of families, and it will not wait for anyone to get ready. It will take you just when it pleases. I think just as many young people die as old ones. I see the names of just as many young people as old people on gravestones. Children, you would not like to die without having sought the Lord at all. Oh, remember – seeking early is the safest way.

Seeking early is the happiest way. If it is so pleasant to have Jesus Christ for a friend, then certainly the sooner you have Him for a friend, the better. You cannot imagine how happy a child's life goes on when his ways please the Lord. Everything seems bright and cheerful. Lessons seem easier and play seems more pleasant. Friends seem kinder and trouble seems less troublesome. Everything in life seems smoother. Dear children, I want you to enjoy all this. Make haste, and do not delay to seek the Lord.

Seeking early is the easiest way. When we have a great deal of work to do, you know there is nothing like beginning early. This is just what you should do about your souls. You should begin early to seek Him who alone can save your soul. People who have got work to do that must be finished before dark take care to get up early in the morning. This is what you should do, dear children, in working about your souls. You should seek the Lord in the morning of life and get your work done before the night of death comes, when no one can work.

Every year that you put it off, you will find it harder work. You will find that there is more to be done and less time to do it. Every year you will find your hearts more stubborn and more unwilling to do what is right. Now your hearts are like young trees – so soft and tender that with the Lord's help, you can bend them in any direction. In a few years, they will be like strong, thick trees – so tough and well-rooted that nothing but a mighty wind can shake them.

Dear children, begin to seek the Lord at once. I want you to have as few difficulties as possible in your journey to heaven.

Consider these things. Consider these things well, and begin early to seek the Lord. It is the safest way, the happiest way, and the easiest way. Try to be like Obadiah, who feared the Lord from his youth (1 Kings 18:12). Try to be like our blessed Lord Jesus Christ Himself, who grew up in favor with God and men (Luke 2:52).

Think of the day when Jesus Christ will come again to this world. He will come again with power and great glory. He will come very suddenly, in an hour when no one expects (Matthew 24:44), like a thief in the night (1 Thessalonians 5:2). He will gather together all who love Him and will take them home to His Father's house to be forever happy. He will leave behind all the idle, wicked, and unbelieving people who have not sought Him, and they will be wretched and miserable forever.

Dear children, Jesus Christ might come very soon. We do not know how soon. How sad it would be to see others taken up to heaven while we are left behind! How dreadful to think, "I could have been taken up too, but I would not seek the Lord!"

Think, too, of the great day of judgment, when all of us will stand before God and give an account of our works. Some of the people who are saved will say then, "I did not begin to seek Jesus Christ until I was forty years old, and I wasted away more than half my life." Others will say, "I did not begin to seek Him until I was twenty, and I wasted many years of my life." But some will be able to say, "I sought the Lord when I was quite young. I can hardly remember the time when I did not love Him."

Dear children, how pleasant it will be for those people to think this! How sweet to feel that they gave the earliest days of their lives to Jesus Christ! How glorious they will appear who have loved their Savior in the beginning of their lives, as well as in the end. May the Lord grant that many of you will be found among them. Oh, seek the Lord early! Seek Him while He may be found (Isaiah 55:6).

Now, dear children, it is time for me to end this section. I might never see you in this world, but we will all meet at the last day of judgment. I do hope you will think about what I have told you about Jesus Christ and your souls. Remember, I want you all to be happy children, and in order to be truly happy, you must love Jesus Christ!

Chapter 7

Boys and Girls Playing

The streets of the city shall be full of boys and girls playing. – Zechariah 8:5

Dear children, the verse above is about things to come. God tells us what there will be one day in the streets of Jerusalem. Jerusalem, you know, is a very famous place. It was the main town of the Jews. It was the city where David and Solomon lived. It was the city where Christ died on the cross and rose again. All boys and girls who read the Bible know something about Jerusalem.

Jerusalem was once a very great and rich town. In all the earth, there was no city like it when the Jews feared God. But the sins of the Jews brought ruin on Jerusalem. It became a poor, decayed, dirty place, and a sorrow to all who see it. But a day will yet come when Jerusalem will once more be a grand and beautiful place – and then the words of the verse will come to pass: *The streets of the city shall be full of boys and girls playing.*

Dear children, there are two things I want you to learn from this verse. God tells us that in the holiest, best days of Jerusalem, there will be boys and girls playing in the streets. He tells us this, and He does not say that it is wrong. Let us see what we can make of this.

God thinks about boys and girls. For one thing, know that God thinks about boys and girls and notices what they do. Not only does He tell us about the men and women of Jerusalem, but He also makes mention of the boys and girls. He tells us that it will be a good time when there are many of them, and that it will be a good time when they play in the streets.

Some people do not care to see children, and they say that there are too many of them in the world. These folks are not like God. The great God in heaven loves children. He knows that there will eventually be no men and women around if there are no children now. He says in Psalm 127:5 that the man is happy who has his quiver full of children! People who do not like boys and girls and who are irritated with them should remember that they were once children themselves.

There is much about children in the Bible. Read the histories of Ishmael, Isaac, Benjamin, Moses, Samuel, and Abijah. Read the proverbs of Solomon and see how often that wise man spoke of children. Read the Gospels and see how Jesus Christ noticed little children and how He took them in His arms and blessed them (Mark 10:16). Read the epistles of the apostle Paul and see how he speaks of children. These things were written for our learning.

Dear children, remember all this. Do not forget it. You are never too young or too little for God to take notice of you. You are never too young or too little to begin thinking of God. Are you old enough to be disobedient? Then be sure that you are old enough to be good. Are you old enough to talk? Then be sure that you are old enough to say your prayers. Are you old enough to learn bad words? Then be sure that you are old enough to learn verses from the Bible. Are you old enough to know and love your father and mother? Then be sure that you are old enough to know and love Jesus, who died to save sinners just like you.

Boys and girls, remember this first great lesson: God takes notice of you. Be sure that you take notice of God.

God allows boys and girls to play. Learn another thing from our verse: God allows boys and girls to play. He does not tell us that the streets of Jerusalem will be full of boys and girls sitting still and silent and not doing anything. He tells us that the boys and girls will be playing, and He teaches us that playing is not wrong. Some people seem to think that children should never play at all. They tell us that all games are sinful and that boys and girls should always look very serious and never laugh or be merry. They make a big mistake when they say this. God tells us that in the good times of Jerusalem, boys and girls will play in the streets.

Therefore, playing in moderation cannot be wrong. Play is appropriate for the age of boys and girls. They cannot be always learning lessons or working. Their minds are not strong enough for this. They are not like older people. They must have some time every day for play and exercise. Play helps children to grow healthy and strong. Their bodies will never be well if they are always sitting still or standing from morning to night. They need all their limbs to be exercised while young if they are to be healthy men and women when they are older. It is natural for children to play. A boy or girl who does not like to play is generally not well.

Play teaches children to be patient, to get along with others, and to put up with disappointments. They cannot always win the game and have their own way. Play makes them active and keen-witted and ready for anything. They cannot succeed in games of skill unless they keep awake.

Play makes boys and girls learn better when it is over. They come back to lessons sharper, quicker, and more clever than if they sat reading and writing all day long. Brains and nerves and minds are all better for play. Play of any kind is better than idleness. Satan always finds some work for idle hands to do! If boys and girls do not have some nice games to play after school, they are quite sure to get into mischief.

Dear children, you see that I am a friend to your playing. I am not ashamed of being so because I see that God approves of it. God allows us to do anything except sin, and play in moderation is not sinful.

Four Pieces of Advice

I will now finish this chapter with four pieces of advice to boys and girls, which I hope they will think about and not forget:

1. **In all your play, remember the eye and ear of God.** He sees and hears everything. Dear children, say nothing that you would not like God to hear.

Do nothing that you would not like God to see.

2. **In all your play, keep your temper.** Be kind, cheerful, unselfish, and good-natured – even if you lose the game. Dear children, never fly into an angry passion. Whatever you play at, keep your temper.

3. **Do not neglect work because of play.** Let all your play help you to learn better and to be a better boy or girl, both at school and home. It is quite true that "all work and no play makes a dull boy," but I believe it is no less true that all play and no work makes a foolish, useless adult!

4. **Never forget, even in your play, that all true happiness comes from Christ.** If you want to be happy, love Christ and make Him your foremost friend. Christ is the giver of light hearts and peaceful minds. The happiest child is the child who loves Christ most.

J. C. Ryle – A Brief Biography

John Charles Ryle was born into a wealthy, affluent, socially elite family on May 10, 1816 – the firstborn son of John Ryle, a banker, and his wife Susanna (Wirksworth) Ryle. As the firstborn, John lived a privileged life and was set to inherit all of his father's estate and pursue a career in Parliament. His future promised to be planned and comfortable with no material needs.

J. C. Ryle attended a private school and then earned academic scholarships to Eton (1828) and the University of Oxford (1834), but he excelled in sports. He particularly made his mark in rowing and cricket. Though his pursuit of sports was short lived, he claimed that they gave him leadership gifts. "It gave me a power of commanding, managing, organizing and directing, seeing through men's capabilities and using every man in the post to which he was best suited, bearing and forbearing, keeping men around me in good temper, which I have found of infinite use on lots of occasions in life, though in very different matters."

In 1837, before graduation, Ryle contracted a serious chest infection, which caused him to turn to the Bible and prayer for the first time in over fourteen years. One Sunday he entered church late as Ephesians 2:8 was being read – slowly, phrase by phrase. John felt the Lord was speaking to him personally, and he claims to have been converted at that moment through the Word without any commentary or sermon.

His biographer wrote, "He came under conviction, was converted, and from that moment to the last recorded syllable of this life, no doubt ever lingered in John's mind that the Word of God was living and powerful, sharper than any two-edged sword."

After graduation from Oxford, John went to London to study law for his career in politics, but in 1841, his father's bank crashed. That was the end of the career in politics, for he had no funding to continue.

In later years, John wrote, "We got up one summer's morning with all the world before us as usual, and went to bed that same night completely and entirely ruined. The immediate consequences were bitter and painful in the extreme, and humiliating to the utmost degree."

And at another time, he said, "The plain fact was there was no one of the family whom it touched more than it did me. My father and mother were no longer young and in the downhill of life; my brothers and sisters, of course, never expected to live at Henbury (the family home) and naturally never thought of it as their house after a certain time. I, on the contrary, as the eldest son, twenty-five, with all the world before me, lost everything, and saw the whole future of my life turned upside down and thrown into confusion."

After this financial ruin from abundance, Ryle was a commoner – all in a day. For the first time in his life, he needed a job. His education qualified him for the clergy, so with his Oxford degree, he was ordained and entered the ministry of the Church of England. He proceeded in a totally different direction with his first assignment in the ministry at Exbury in Hampshire, but it was a rural area riddled with disease. His recurring lung infection made a difficult couple of years until he was transferred to St. Thomas in Winchester. With his commanding presence, passionately held principles, and warm disposition, John's congregation grew so large and strong it needed different accommodations.

Ryle accepted a position at that time in Helmington, Suffolk, where he had much time to read theologians like Wesley, Bunyan, Knox, Calvin, and Luther. He was a contemporary of Charles Spurgeon, Dwight Moody, George Mueller, and Hudson Taylor. He lived in the age of Dickens, Darwin, and the American Civil War. All of these influenced Ryle's understanding and theology.

His writing career began from the tragedy of the Great Yarmouth suspension bridge. On May 9, 1845, a large crowd gathered for the official grand opening festivities, but the bridge collapsed and more than a hundred people plunged into the water and drowned. The incident shocked the whole country but it led Ryle to write his first tract. He spoke of life's uncertainties and God's sure provision of salvation through Jesus Christ. Thousands of copies were sold.

That same year, he married Matilda Plumptre, but she died after only two years, leaving him with an infant daughter. In 1850, he married Jessie Walker, but she had a lingering sickness, which caused Ryle to care for her and their growing family (three sons and another daughter) for ten years until she died. In 1861, he was transferred to Stradbroke, Suffolk, where he married Henrietta Clowes.

Stradbroke, Suffolk, was Ryle's last parish, and he gained a reputation for his straightforward preaching and evangelism. Besides his travelling and preaching, he spent time writing. He wrote more than 300 pamphlets, tracts, and books. His books include *Expository Thoughts on the Gospels* (7 Volumes, 1856-1869), *Principles for Churchmen* (1884), *Home Truths, Knots Untied, Old Paths,* and *Holiness.*

His *Christian Leaders of the Eighteenth Century* (1869) is described as having "short, pithy sentences, compelling logic and penetrating insight into spiritual power." This seems to be the case with most of his writing as he preached and wrote with five main guidelines: (1) Have a clear view of the subject, (2) Use simple words, (3) Use a simple style of composition, (4) Be direct, and (5) Use plenty of anecdotes and illustrations.

In all of his success with writing, he used the royalties to pay his father's debts. He may have felt indebted to that financial ruin, for he said, "I have not the least doubts, it was all for the best. If I had not been ruined, I should never have been a clergyman, never preached a sermon, or written a tract or book."

In spite of all of the trials that Ryle experienced – financial ruin, loss of three wives, his own poor health – he learned several life lessons. First, care and tend to your own family. Second, swim against the tide when you need to. He was evangelical before it was popular and he held to principles of Scripture: justification by faith alone, substitutionary atonement, the Trinity, and preaching. Third, model Christian attitudes toward your opponents. Fourth, learn and understand church history. Important benefits come from past generations. Fifth, serve in old age; "die in the harness." And, sixth, persevere through your trials.

These were life principles that Ryle learned as he lived his life, as he preached, as he wrote, and as he spread the gospel. He was forever a supporter of evangelism and a critic of ritualism.

J. C. Ryle was recommended by Prime Minister Benjamin Disraeli to be Bishop of Liverpool in 1880 where he then worked to build churches and mission halls to reach the whole city. He retired in 1900 at the age of 83 and died later that year. His successor described him as "a man of granite with a heart of a child."

G. C. B. Davies said "a commanding presence and fearless advocacy of his principles were combined with a kind and understanding attitude in his personal relationships."[1]

---

[1] Sources:
William P. Farley, "J. C. Ryle: A 19th-century Evangelical," *Enrichment Journal, http://enrichmentjournal.ag.org/200604/200604_120_jcryle.cfm.*

"J. C. Ryle," *The Banner of Truth, https://banneroftruth.org/us/about/banner-authors/j-c-ryle/.*

"J. C. Ryle," *Theopedia, https://www.theopedia.com/john-charles-ryle.*

David Holloway, "J. C. Ryle – The Man, The Minister and The Missionary," *Bible Bulletin Board, http://www.biblebb.com/files/ryle/j_c_ryle.htm.*

Other Similar Titles

ANEKO
PRESS

The Duties of Parents, by J. C. Ryle

In *The Duties of Parents*, J. C. Ryle presents seventeen simple and yet profound responsibilities of Christian parents. Nothing new is contained in this little volume, yet what is presented has the potential to change future generations both now and for eternity. Learn how to shepherd your children; learn how to utilize the most significant key of all – love; and learn first and foremost how to present and represent Christ to your children. As you read this book, expect to find yourself both challenged and excited to begin a wonderful, appropriate, and growing relationship with the most wonderful gift God can give us in our lifetime – our dear children.

Available where books are sold.

Come Ye Children,
by Charles H. Spurgeon

Teaching children things of the Lord is an honor and a high calling. Children have boundless energy and may appear distracted, but they are capable of understanding biblical truths even adults have a hard time grasping. Children's minds are easily impressed with new thoughts, whether good or bad, and will remember many of their young lessons for the rest of their life. Adults and churches tend to provide entertainment to occupy the children, but children ought to have our undivided attention. Jesus said, let the little children come to me. They were worthy of His time and devotion, and they are worthy of ours.

Available where books are sold.

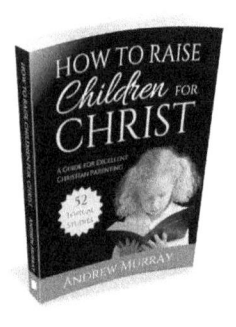

How to Raise Children for Christ,
by Andrew Murray

This book is different from most books on raising children. It is a plea for the parents to truly know and walk with God – for them to love God and His Word. In the correct order, focusing first on the parents, Andrew Murray then urges parents to sincerely and consistently love their children and in all tenderness and gentleness teach them as God also teaches us.

Available where books are sold.

Heaven,
by Dwight L. Moody

The goal of this book is to whet your appetite for heaven. A careful look at Scripture reveals that heaven is what every born-again believer is longing for. Our time on earth is only in a temporary dwelling place, and heaven is the true home of all God's children. A study of heaven can change how you approach each day, and even how you view others around you. As real as this life is, we are assured that heaven is just as real. While we must not neglect our present God-given duties, we must at the same time be preparing for our future home and should even be looking forward with great anticipation to our eternal home.

Available where books are sold.

Daniel, Man of God,
by Dwight L. Moody

God will exalt us when the time is right. We needn't try to promote ourselves; we needn't struggle for position. Let God put us where He wants us and let us be true to God. It is better for a man to be right with God, even if he holds no great earthly position. It is honest and humble men whom God will promote, if He so desires.

This study illustrates what Daniel did, and also what Daniel didn't do, which caught the attention of God and kings alike. Few are the men in history of Daniel's caliber, even though the principles he followed can be implemented by all. Are you ready to be a truly great man, one that will cause God and men to take notice?

Available where books are sold.

God Is My Boss, Shirley Carlson

Champions of the Great Commission is a series of stories of One Mission Society missionaries and partners that have answered God's call to fulfill the Great Commission—to go and make disciples of all nations (Matthew 28:19-20). These men and women have spent their lives serving him, sharing the love of Jesus in amazing ways with people all around the world.

Stanley Tam, born in 1915, is a successful businessman with a strong faith in God and great generosity. He has given millions of dollars to One Mission Society to help hundreds of thousands of people hear the Good News of Jesus. *God Is My Boss* tells the story of how God used an ordinary man to do extraordinary things when he literally gave his business to the Lord.

Available where books are sold.

The Overcoming Life,
by Dwight L. Moody

Are you an overcomer? Or, are you plagued by little sins that easily beset you? Even worse, are you failing in your Christian walk, but refuse to admit and address it? No Christian can afford to dismiss the call to be an overcomer. The earthly cost is minor; the eternal reward is beyond measure.

Dwight L. Moody uses stories and humor to bring to light the essential principles of successful Christian living. Each aspect of overcoming is looked at from a practical and understandable angle. The solution Moody presents for our problems is not religion, rules, or other outward corrections. Instead, he takes us to the heart of the matter and prescribes biblical, God-given remedies for every Christian's life. Get ready to embrace genuine victory for today, and joy for eternity.

Available where books are sold.

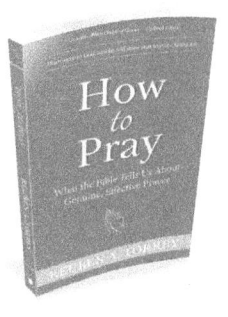

How to Pray,
by Reuben A. Torrey

Great revivals always begin first in the hearts of a few men and women whom God arouses by His Spirit to believe in Him as a living God, as a God who answers prayer, and upon whose heart He lays a burden from which no rest can be found except in persistent crying unto God.

May God use this book to inspire many who are currently prayerless, or nearly so, to pray earnestly. May God stir up your own heart to be one of those burdened to pray, and to pray until God answers.

Available where books are sold.

Life on the Family Farm, by Tom Heck

"You are the most God-gifted writer I've ever had," Tom's college professor told him. However, Tom quit college; his love of farming drew him back to the farm. Thirty years later, Tom picked up the pen again, drawing readers into farming adventures with him. In these exciting and uplifting true stories, he shares his love of farming, family, and God. His unique writing style brings the reader right alongside him and his family as they work on their northern Wisconsin dairy farm.

From quotes like "Dad, I really enjoyed fixing that with you" to "She's a dead cow don't call me anymore," these engaging stories will keep you turning the pages to read one story, then another. As you do, you will be blessed as so many others have been.

Available where books are sold.

Pilgrim's Progress,
by John Bunyan

Often disguised as something that would help him, evil accompanies Christian on his journey to the Celestial City. As you walk with him, you'll begin to identify today's many religious pitfalls. These are presented by men such as Pliable, who turns back at the Slough of Despond; and Ignorance, who believes he's a true follower of Christ when he's really only trusting in himself. Each character represented in this allegory is intentionally and profoundly accurate in its depiction of what we see all around us, and unfortunately, what we too often see in ourselves. But while Christian is injured and nearly killed, he eventually prevails to the end. So can you.

Available where books are sold.

CPSIA information can be obtained
at www.ICGtesting.com
Printed in the USA
BVHW020241270323
661201BV00012B/326

9 781622 457847